MEN AT
WORK

DAN JOHNSON & JON TICE

Regular Baptist Press
1300 North Meacham Road
Schaumburg, Illinois 60173-4806

MEN AT WORK
© 2004
Regular Baptist Press • Schaumburg, Illinois
1-800-727-4440 • www.regularbaptistpress.org
Printed in U.S.A.
All rights reserved
RBP5317 • ISBN: 1-59402-030-2

MEN AT
WORK

CONTENTS

YOUR WORK

When you think about how to be a godly man, do you think about your job? Not many people think of "work" as being a characteristic of godliness, and yet it is. God works, and God created work! Genesis 1 describes one of God's significant work weeks. His work on earth began with the creation of the world, continued with the task of separating the light from the darkness, included the finest details imprinted on the first man and woman, and ended with a day of rest.

Creation was far from God's only work. God demonstrated His ultimate work through Christ's death, burial, and resurrection, which brings salvation to man (1 Corinthians 15:3, 4). Christ is currently working to build a home in Heaven for all His children (John 14:2, 3). Ephesians 2:10 describes every child of God as God's "workmanship."

As creatures made in the image of God, we are made to work. Adam's first job description included naming all the animals and subduing the earth. And you thought you had a lot to do!

When sin entered the world, work became difficult. Genesis 3:19 states, "In the sweat of thy face shalt thou eat bread, till thou return unto the ground." In light of this curse brought upon humanity, men need God's help and one another's encouragement in order to become God's men at work.

Most men will spend almost one hundred thousand hours in their lifetimes working at a job. That is an enormous investment of time and energy. The goal of this study guide is to help men experience God's plan **for** work rather than merely enduring the time **at** work.

1
PURPOSE AND VALUE OF WORK

Why do you work? Imagine going to your mailbox and finding a letter informing you that a distant relative has died and has left you ten million dollars. Stop and think, *What would I do about my job?*

Some men would take a couple days off work to develop an investment and spending plan. Many would quit their jobs altogether. What would you do?

How we put bread on our tables is a huge part of life. Most men are serious about their responsibility to provide for their families. However, God's plan for work is deeper than work merely being a means to pay bills. God has planted into the heart of all men the need to work.

Let's take a look at how work originated. The first few chapters of the Bible show God at work.

1. The word "work" first appears in Genesis 2:2 and 3. What stands out to you about God's work in these verses? _____

_____

Many people dream of the day when they won't have to go to work any longer. How many of us have stood in a long line, waiting to pay for gasoline or milk, and have heard some guy boldly proclaim, "If I hit the jackpot, I'll quit my job so fast it will make my boss's head spin," and then watched as he bought twenty dollars worth of lottery tickets? This scenario might hit a little closer to home with some men: eagerly counting down the days to retirement as a time "when work will be no more," or so we think. These attitudes are evidence of the fact that many men have never discovered the true point of work.

The Bible teaches that work includes three primary goals: provision, production, and purpose. The challenge is to find and maintain a balance within these three areas of work. Have you noticed how tough it is to find balance?

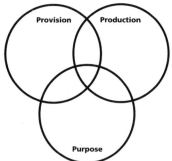

Area 1: Provision

One reason why we work is to put food on the table and pay the bills. The man who desires to follow God must move beyond seeing only his own needs to gaining a vision for the greater needs of God's work. This progression could be viewed in this way:

Impoverished	**Worldly Provision**	**Biblical Provider**
Unable to provide for oneself	Providing only for oneself	Providing for oneself and God's work

Place a mark on the line where you view yourself today.

2. On day six of creation God created man and woman. Look at the account in Genesis 1:26–31. In Genesis 1:28 and 29 God gave Adam and Eve jobs. What were they? _____

_____

_____

Other Bible passages expand upon this principle of provision.

3. What steps did the apostle Paul list in 1 Thessalonians 4:11 and 12 as ways to prevent being in need? _____

Not be a burden, have worth & provision

make ambition

not all about work

4. What warning does 1 Timothy 5:8 give about not providing for one's own? _____

_____

_____

_____

5. Who else should we provide for according to Ephesians 4:28?

_____

_____

_____

Area 2: Production

The second goal of work is production. What kind of lives would we have today if Henry Ford, Thomas Edison, Benjamin Franklin, or Bill Gates had been lazy?

God instructed Adam to cultivate the earth. Think of all the productivity it took to fulfill God's command. We work to produce those items that improve our effort to "cultivate" the earth.

Just as God stepped back after each day of creation and said, "It is good," we desire to step back after a job is done and say, "It is good!" A man who works all day and feels he has accomplished nothing is frustrated by that lack of production. God wants us to be productive, and He may even navigate us through jobs in order to bring us to a place where our presence and impact are needed.

6. In the following passages in Genesis, what "production" did God expect from Adam?

  • Genesis 1:28 _____

  _____

  _____

  • Genesis 2:15 _____

  _____

  _____

  • Genesis 2:16, 17 _____

  _____

  _____

  • Genesis 2:19, 20 _____

  _____

  _____

7. What does your job produce that can improve efforts to "cultivate" the earth? _____

  _____

  _____

Area 3: Purpose

The third area of work is purpose. Jesus said in Matthew 18:11

that He came "to save that which was lost." Paul's mission was to preach the good news about Jesus (1 Corinthians 9:16). Moses' purpose was to lead Israel to the Promised Land (Exodus 3:10). Joseph's purpose was to organize Egypt in preparation for a famine (Genesis 38—41; 45:5). Nehemiah's purpose was to rebuild Jerusalem (Nehemiah 2:1–5). The greater the purpose that a job has, the greater fulfillment that job brings.

8. What attitude did Jesus have about the work He did?

• John 4:34 _____

_____

_____

_____

• John 9:4 _____

_____

_____

_____

• John 17:4 _____

_____

_____

_____

When God defined man's job on the earth as "be fruitful, and multiply, and . . . subdue [the earth]" (Genesis 1:28), God was saying that Adam's "job" mattered. Every morally responsible job has some meaningful purpose in God's process. So your job matters too!

Jesus knew His work was valuable because it pleased His Father. Throughout His earthly life Jesus modeled these balanced characteristics of work, and He continues to do so. Jesus **provides** for our eternal need of salvation and for our everyday needs (John 3:16; Philippians

4:19). Jesus demonstrates the goal of **production** through the church (Matthew 16:18). Jesus demonstrates the **purpose** of His work in us (John 15:8–11; Ephesians 5:27).

9. What do Colossians 3:23 and 24 teach about whom you are to please with your work? _____

_____

_____

The attitude you have about your job is important to God. Whether you are a factory worker, a salesperson, a missionary, a grocer, a computer technician, a doctor, a pastor, a lawyer, a mechanic, or an office manager, your work matters to God! When what we do is powered by the motivation to please God as our true employer, the provision, production, and purpose of our work combine to greatly reward us. God seems to want at least two things in the heart of a person as it relates to his job: (1) right actions concerning the job, and (2) the right attitude about the job.

Look again at the balance required in the three areas of work. The pursuit of this balance as modeled by Christ will unlock God's unbelievable, fulfilling potential for your work.

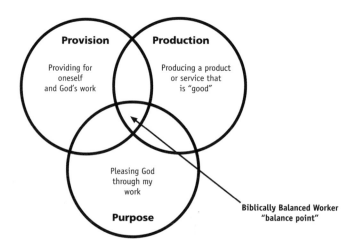

Heart Check

Work is important to God.

Work helps you be a **provider**.

Work helps you serve others.

Work enables you to be **productive**.

Work has **purpose** in life.

Place on X where you are on the balanced work diagram (p. 14).

What actions or attitudes can you take at work to move you toward
the balance point? _____

_____

_____

_____

Verses for Meditation

"And whatsoever ye do, do it heartily, as to the Lord, and not
unto men; Knowing that of the Lord ye shall receive the reward
of the inheritance: for ye serve the Lord Christ" (Colossians
3:23, 24).

2
PASSION AND ACHIEVEMENT

D o you presently live in the same town where you grew up? Many high school graduates get an "itch," convincing them that the best possible future will involve a new zip code. Sometimes this desire may simply be a symptom of the-grass-is-greener-on-the-other-side-of-the-fence syndrome. At other times it represents a calling in our lives to accomplish our greatest potential.

One interesting characteristic of many heroes of the Bible is that in order to get to the place of greatest impact in their lives, they had to step out in faith and embrace a new calling. Notice this progression.

Where God wants me

Faith

Where I am

1. Do you currently have the employment you really want? _____

   _____

2. What do you like about your present occupation? _____

   _____

   _____

   _____

   _____

3. What don't you like about your job? _____

   _____

   _____

   _____

   _____

4. If you could chose any career without the concern of providing
   for your family, what would you be doing today? _____

   _____

   _____

   _____

The Bible is full of career-progression stories. Each one had a
starting point and required a **faith step** that led the character to a
place of impact.

5. Look up the passages listed for each character and note the three
   areas for each character. The first one is filled in for you.

	START	FAITH STEP	PLACE OF IMPACT
Joseph	Genesis 39:1–4, 9, 10 *Potiphar's servant*	Genesis 39:20—40:23 *Faithful in prison*	Genesis 41:38–45 *Advisor to Pharaoh*
Moses	Exodus 3:1, 2	Exodus 3:10; 4:1–13	Exodus 7:1–7
Joshua	Numbers 13:1–3, 8	Numbers 14:5–10	Joshua 1:1–9
Matthew	Matthew 9:9	Matthew 9:9–13	Matthew 10:1–3

Paul's Example

Paul (formerly Saul) was first a Jewish religious terrorist who tried to get rid of the followers of Jesus. The Lord met Saul on the road to Damascus and changed his life's direction (Acts 9). Paul's new life included returning to tent making (Acts 18:3) and becoming an evangelist (Colossians 4:3, 4), an apostle (Colossians 1:1), and a theology teacher (Acts 18:11). In Philippians 3 Paul described several qualities that guided his journey from where he was to where God wanted him. Commitment, ambition, and contentment enabled Paul to make a great impact with his life.

Commitment

Commitment is the choice to be faithful in our current responsibilities. Commitment means resisting the temptation to become lazy where we are while being enamored with where we want to go. It is our commitment to God that will make even the most difficult job bearable. Without this one commitment to faithfulness, life becomes a jumbled series of ultimately meaningless events that may produce temporary distraction but never sustaining value.

6. Read Philippians 3:1–16. How did Paul describe his background (vv. 4–6)? _____

_____

_____

_____

7. What was his goal in life (v. 10)? _____

_____

_____

_____

8. What commitment did Paul describe in Philippians 3:13 and 14?

_____

_____

_____

Paul's focus was Christ, Who must be the focus of any person who wants to follow God. Without a spiritual focus on Jesus Christ, your life will not produce the meaning you want from it.

Philippians 3:13 and 14 also apply to our work life because commitment is the path to achievement in any pursuit in life. In *The Scottish Himalayan Expedition*, W. H. Murray explained: "Until one is committed, there is hesitancy, the chance to draw back, always ineffectiveness. Concerning all acts of initiative there is one elementary truth, the ignorance of which kills countless ideas and splendid plans: that the moment one definitely commits oneself, then Providence moves too. All sorts of things occur to help one that would never otherwise have occurred. A whole stream of events issues from the decision, raising in one's favor all manner of unforeseen incidents and meetings and material assistance, which no man could have dreamed would have come his way" (John Roger and Peter McWilliams, *Life 101* [Los Angeles: Prelude Press, 1991], 225).

9. Read again Philippians 3:13 and 14 and ask yourself, How would I apply Paul's attitude of commitment toward my current job?

_____

_____

_____

Ambition

Ambition is the desire to do well in our current assignment and to be eligible to progress to a higher level. In Philippians 3:13 and 14 Paul defined a powerful plan for growth. Ambition views past victories and successes not as completion but as momentum and motivation for the next step. Looking back should lead us to look ahead, so that we conclude, "What has happened in the past has set me up for the next step." These next steps in following God are always "faith steps." God loves it when we walk with Him by faith (Hebrews 11:6).

10. How has a past job or experience prepared you for what you are doing now? _____

_____

_____

_____

11. Describe how you are motivated to continue to improve your performance on your job. _____

_____

_____

Contentment

Contentment is internal peace that supercedes external circumstances. Regardless of how far up the corporate ladder you climb or don't climb, you can always demonstrate contentment. Philippians 4:10–13 describes this contentment. Remember that Philippians is one of the letters Paul wrote from prison while he suffered some of the worst possible "life conditions" imaginable. Yet he urged us to be content.

In Philippians 4:11 the word "learned" conveys the idea that contentment is not a natural trait, but one that has to be developed over time. The word "content" is also fascinating. The Greek word literally means "self-sufficient." It carries the idea of having sufficient resources on the inside so that a person doesn't need to rely upon what's outside for happiness.

12. What is the source of this inner sufficiency (Philippians 4:13)?

_____

Paul was a man at peace because he relied on the sufficiency of Christ. This peace enabled Paul to say that he was content whether in a prison or a palace. The teaching of Philippians 4:13 reminds us that we can do anything through the power of Jesus Christ. A godly man rises to the challenge to maintain a healthy balance between the passion to achieve (commitment + ambition) and contentment.

We might picture this balance in the following formula:

Commitment + Ambition + Contentment = IMPACT

Heart Check

Describe the level of your commitment to a desire to pursue God's purpose for your life, including your employment. _____

_____

_____

_____

_____

_____

_____

_____

Ask yourself, Am I dependent on my job to bring me the peace I am looking for in life? _____

Evaluate your life in this area: In both my work and my life away from work, how do I show that I am learning contentment?

_____

_____

_____

Verses for Meditation

"Brethren, I count not myself to have apprehended: but this one thing I do, forgetting those things which are behind, and reaching forth unto those things which are before" (Philippians 3:13); "I can do all things through Christ which strengtheneth me" (Philippians 4:13).

3
WHERE DO I FIT?
CAREER PATH

Thirty years ago a man commonly worked for the same company most or all of his career. Today many men will work for numerous employers over the course of their working years.

Check which of the following descriptions best identifies where you are today.

❑ I have known what I wanted to do since I was young, and I have never wavered. Today I am still at it and wouldn't want to do anything else.

❑ I had a clear view of what career I wanted to pursue, and everything went great until I started working at it. Now I feel stuck and frustrated.

❑ I had a clear view of what career I wanted to pursue, but it never happened. So today, I'm working at something else and loving it.

❑ I have never had a clear idea about a career, and today I am more confused about what I need to be doing than ever before.

Have you ever taken an aptitude test? Many people take tests designed to gauge IQs or personalities. Perhaps you may have taken a vocational aptitude test to discover what career would best suit you. While those tests may be helpful, several Biblical principles are even more important.

Many men try to find where they fit in the marketplace, sometimes because their company forces such a search and sometimes because their occupation is not a true "fit." Consider these five steps either to affirm that you fit where you are or to help you find your fit.

Workplace Checklist

Step 1: Spiritual sensitivity

A successful businessman said to me, "Every bad decision I've ever made, I've made while walking in the flesh." In stark contrast to "walking in the flesh," the goal of a Christian man in his work is to live a Spirit-filled existence through a committed relationship with Jesus Christ.

To be Spirit-filled is to be Spirit-controlled. In Ephesians 5:18 Paul drew a contrasting analogy between drunkenness and being Spirit-filled.

In our culture if authorities arrest a person for driving while drunk, the violation is referred to as "DUI," or "driving under the influence." In other words, the alcohol so influences that person's behavior that speech is slurred, inhibitions are lowered, and reactions are slowed. The influence of alcohol is dramatic.

The influence of the Holy Spirit is much more dramatic. Paul chose to use this contrasting analogy to exhort us to live under the influence of the Holy Spirit. If we follow this exhortation, our speech, our reactions, and our general behavior will be affected.

How can we know if we are "LUI," or "living under the influence" of the Holy Spirit? In a suspected DUI, a police officer may pull a vehicle over if he or she suspects that the driver has been drinking. The officer will evaluate the suspect by asking the person to touch his or her nose or to walk a straight line. The individual may even need to blow into a device that gauges the alcohol content in one's blood. A similar test ought to be personally administered for every man who desires to live under the influence of Christ. He must ask himself, Am I filled with the Holy Spirit in my workplace?

Read Ephesians 5:18 and Galatians 5:22 and 23.

1. According to Galatians 5:22 and 23, what are the nine indications that one is under the influence of the Holy Spirit? _____

   _____

   _____

   _____

2. Rate yourself in each of the following areas:

Love

- Is my life marked by a selfless determination to bring about the best in the people around me?

   OR

- Do I live selfishly, pursuing and pushing my preferences and my agenda, regardless of how it may affect or even hurt others?

Joy

- Do I portray an inner pleasantness and positive outlook about what God has done and will do in my life?

   OR

- Do I live with a gloomy, negative, downcast view of life?

Peace

- Do I possess an inner tranquility, recognizing that regardless of what happens around me, God is always in control and will lead me through? Do I show that I trust God?

   OR

- Am I persistently stressed by worry and anxiety? Do I fear that if a certain plan doesn't work, if I don't figure out the problem, or if my plan isn't accepted, then everything is going to fall apart?

Patience (Longsuffering)

- Am I marked by a willingness to wait, to endure challenging circumstances and challenging people?

OR

- Am I quick to judge others or to run away from anything difficult or unpleasant?

Kindness (Gentleness)

- Is my demeanor with other people positive and helpful? Am I sensitive to the needs of other people?

OR

- Am I often critical and calloused toward others?

Goodness

- Do I have a desire to be around and participate in that which is of moral value and excellence? Do I have a way of always seeing the bright side?

OR

- Am I a person who usually sees the dark side? Do I frequently focus on that which is morally evil by finding a way to pursue impurity through my thoughts and/or actions?

Faithfulness (Faith)

- Do I have a track record of sticking with the positive pursuits in life during good times and bad times? Do I stick with people during their ups and downs?

OR

- Am I characterized by jumping in with both feet when it benefits me but pulling the plug when it costs me more energy, time, or money than I want to spend?

Gentleness (Meekness)

- Are my strengths purposefully directed?

OR

- Am I a "bull in a china shop," causing more damage than good?

Self-Control (Temperance)

- Do I demonstrate the willingness to tell myself no? Do I deny my fleshly desires?

OR

- Do I chase everything I want? Do I insist on getting my way?

We all will fall short on the checklist of the fruit of the Spirit. Most men find themselves desirous of circling the second choice under each heading because of the battle for consistency in these areas of life. The hard question is, Do you see this kind of fruit growing in your life right now? This growth has nothing to do with whether or not you like your job or current circumstances surrounding your work. This has everything to do with personal growth.

If you are growing, then you recognize that God knows more about making you effective than you do. Once you realize that He is the One in charge of your life, then the great question for you is . . .

Step 2: What are my natural abilities?

Your ability to work with wood or to understand computers is not an accident; it is part of the fabric that God weaves into you to bring creativity and excitement into your life. In the Old Testament when God was looking for someone to build the tabernacle, He didn't go to the priests to look for a capable craftsman. Moses found a man with some natural abilities to do the job.

3. According to Exodus 31:1–6, who gives skill and craftsmanship?

_____

4. Read Exodus 35:30–35, noticing especially verse 34. What else did God place in the heart of this skilled craftsman?_____

_____

_____

A third step is to consider seriously the answer to the following question:

Step 3: What is my burden?

Psalm 37:4 states, "Delight thyself also in the LORD; and he shall give thee the desires of thine heart." When you delight in the Lord, then God will place His desires on your heart. Your place of employment and the desire of your heart should be linked. It is Biblically appropriate to ask the following questions: "What am I good at?" "What do I enjoy?" "What do I want to do?" Paul told Timothy, "If a man desire the office of a bishop, he desireth a good work" (1 Timothy 3:1), indicating that the burden of a person's heart has a great deal to do with a person's work life.

5. Take a moment to think about the job you have always wanted. What is it? Go ahead; write it down. _____

_____

_____

_____

6. Circle a response to the following questions.

Do you have a burden for your current job?

YES   NO   UNSURE

If not, could you gain a burden for this job?

YES   NO   UNSURE

Should you consider a job that more closely fits your burden?

YES   NO   UNSURE

Step 4: What do my mentors recommend?

Are you seeking advice from people whom you trust, those who have your best interest at heart? Solomon wrote, "In the multitude of counsellors there is safety" (Proverbs 11:14); and "He that hearkeneth unto counsel is wise" (Proverbs 12:15).

Paul, Timothy's spiritual mentor, wrote in 2 Timothy 1:6 and 7, "Stir up the gift of God, which is in thee by the putting on of my hands. For God hath not given us the spirit of fear; but of power, and of love, and of a sound mind." The phrase "by the putting on of my hands" does not mean that Paul gave Timothy his spiritual gift. We believe the phrase simply means that Paul recognized and wanted to affirm the fact that Timothy was, in fact, gifted for this kind of work. The input of godly people in your life will help you make wise decisions. Make sure that you have talked with several individuals who know you well and that you have prayed and sought God's direction before you make any life-changing decision. Having done so, proceed forward by faith.

Step 5: What opportunities are there for me to discover?

Opportunity comes when you combine

Step 1: the Spirit-filled life;

Step 2: your natural abilities;

Step 3: the desire of your heart; and

Step 4: the godly counsel of others who can lead you to the action you need to take.

As you study your current job, you may discover that you are exactly where you need to be. On the other hand, God may be working in your heart, leading you to consider pursuing a different job or beginning a second career. Lesson 4, "Job Choice," will explore these decisions in greater detail.

Heart Check

Ask yourself, Where am I?

Are you participating, practicing, and becoming responsible in your current occupation?

Are you considering moving on to some other employment?

Which of the following actions should you take?

- ❏ Live the Spirit-filled life at work
- ❏ Sign up for a technical class at a community college
- ❏ Volunteer for additional responsibilities
- ❏ Continue to read and sharpen my work skills
- ❏ Update my résumé
- ❏ Talk to my counselors about my desire
- ❏ Check job postings at my current employment, in the classified section of a newspaper, or on the Internet
- ❏ Start my own business
- ❏ Other _____

Verse for Meditation

"Delight thyself also in the LORD; and he shall give thee the desires of thine heart" (Psalm 37:4).

4
WHERE DO I FIT?
JOB CHOICE

Within a given career, an individual usually has a number of choices to make. For instance, a plumber must choose either to work independently or for a general contractor. If he chooses to work for a contractor, he must use discretion in his choice. If the plumber starts his own company, should he hire other plumbers to work for him?

How do you know the will of God for *your* life? Our last lesson may have caused you to rethink your career. We believe that most men, at one time or another, wonder, *Did I choose the right career? Am I currently in the right job? Would I like work better if I were doing something else?* If a person truly desires to follow God's plan for his life, these questions may lead him to another thought, *How can I know the direction of God's will about my job?*

1. What one thing is common to each of the following situations: Abraham's leaving his family (Genesis 12:1); Moses' burning bush experience (Exodus 3:1–3); and Joshua's encounter with the Angel of the Lord (Joshua 5:13–15)? _____

_____

_____

Although our lives may not be as dramatic as these Biblical examples, we have the written Word of God, the Bible, to guide us in discerning God's will.

The following five steps will help you make a decision concerning the right employment.

Step 1: Follow God's direct will.

God's will is not discovered by chance but through obedience to specific instructions in God's Word concerning His will for our lives. Note what the following passages teach about God's will.

2. According to Psalm 40:8, where can a person find God's will?

_____

In other words, look in the Word to find God's will.

3. What is God's will for every person (2 Peter 3:9)? _____

_____

_____

4. According to Ephesians 5:17 and 18, with Whom does God want Christians to be filled? _____

_____

5. What is God's will for our moral character (1 Thessalonians 4:3, 4)?

_____

_____

6. How does God want us to respond to the authorities in our lives (1 Peter 2:13–15)? _____

_____

7. In what way does God want us to respond to our suffering (1 Peter 4:14–19)? _____

_____

_____

_____

8. What does James 4:13–16 teach concerning how Christians are to view personal plans? _____

_____

_____

_____

When determining God's will for our lives—the path that God approves—Christians must first look to the Bible. No one will find God's will if he is living outside the Biblical expressions of God's will. After ensuring that a person's life is aligned with specific statements concerning God's will, the next step is to consider Biblical principles that indirectly address the issue at hand.

Step 2: Check Biblical principles.

Consider these questions as you seek to determine God's will.

- What Biblical principles apply to making this type of decision?

- Is the purpose, product, or goal of the company inconsistent with Biblical truth?

- Does the work environment involve consistent and strong temptations to sin?

- What will the decision require of my family life?

- How will the decision affect my wife? (Check 1 Peter 3:7.)

- What impact will it make on my children? (Check Ephesians 6:4.)

- Is my primary motivation personal prosperity or pleasing God? (Check 1 Timothy 6:6–10.)

These questions will help narrow your options and, in many cases, provide a clear answer.

Step 3: Ask for God's wisdom.

9. What does James 1:5–7 teach us about how to pray? _____

_____

_____

_____

10. What additional principles concerning prayer are found in James 4:3 and 5:16? _____

_____

_____

_____

Accept no substitute for obeying God's command to ask for help! It is in asking that you realize your dependence upon God. You can't rely on your own strength. But you can, with God's wisdom, be and do what He wants.

Step 4: Seek godly counsel.

Review Lesson 3, step 4, on page 30.

Step 5: Take action in faith.

11. Read Hebrews 11:1 and 6. Explain the importance of faith in the Christian life. _____

_____

_____

_____

12. Read Romans 14:23. What is the principle in this verse? _____

_____

_____

You will not have a "burning bush" experience like Moses (Exodus 3:1—4:17) or be called in the night like young Samuel (1 Samuel 3:3–15), but God has provided a faith-building tool, the Bible, that will lead you. Whether you remain in your current job or move to a different one, be convinced that "this is where God wants me right now."

Heart Check

Which step from this lesson needs some more attention from you?

_____

_____

What action should you take? _____

_____

_____

_____

Verse for Meditation

"I delight to do thy will, O my God: yea, thy law is within my heart" (Psalm 40:8).

5
SUCCESS

Walk into any bookstore or library and you will find shelves full of strategies to make your life a success. Our culture most often views success as "attaining some measure of money, fame, power and self-fulfillment—and then looking the part" (Steve Turner and Dennis Haach, *The Rest of Success* [Nashville: Thomas Nelson Publishers, Inc., 1991], 50).

A dictionary definition of success is "the achievement of something desired, planned, or attempted" *(American Heritage Dictionary of the English Language).*

How does God view success? Clearly God viewed Jesus as the ultimate success when God proclaimed, "Thou art my beloved Son, in whom I am well pleased" (Mark 1:11).

By studying the life of Christ we can learn important principles concerning success.

Success is not PROFIT.

Jesus is the ultimate example of success, but He was never financially rich.

1. What do we learn about Jesus from Matthew 8:20? _____

_____

The Bible says that "though he [Jesus] was rich, yet for your sakes he became poor" (2 Corinthians 8:9).

Success is not POWER.

Jesus is the ultimate example of success, but He had no political or corporate power. As God He had authority, as evidenced in the power of His words and the impact of His life (Mark 1:22).

Success is not POSITION.

Jesus is the ultimate example of success, but "he came unto his own, and his own received him not" (John 1:11).

Jesus viewed success as the accomplishment of His intended work on the cross for the salvation of mankind, which is what led Him to say on the cross, "It is finished" (John 19:30).

What success IS

Psalm 1:3 describes the successful Christian as "a tree planted by the rivers of water, that bringeth forth his fruit in his season; his leaf also shall not wither; and whatsoever he doeth shall prosper."

2. According to Psalm 1:1 and 2, what propels a man toward achieving God-styled success? _____

_____

_____

_____

The Bible uses a number of words to convey the idea of achieving our God-instilled potential. Words like "blessed," "reward," "favour," "happy," "greatest" are used as synonyms for success. God's idea of success is most clearly seen in the examples of men in the Bible who had great character and true achievement.

3. Look at these key passages and write how the Bible describes each man's success.

	The Man	**The Success**
Genesis 12:1–3		
Genesis 39:2		
1 Kings 3:6–15		
Matthew 11:11		

Biblical success is fully achieving the potential that God has placed within us so that He is pleased with our lives.

Nehemiah's Example

Nehemiah is another Biblical example of success. He was a Jew, yet he was the cupbearer (a food and wine taster who made sure the king's food was not poisoned) to King Artaxerxes, ruler of the kingdom of Persia. He heard through other Jewish captives that Jerusalem was literally falling apart. The walls were broken down, the gates were torn off, and the people were demoralized and beaten.

Nehemiah had a burden to see the walls of Jerusalem rebuilt, and he believed God could use him to do it. Nehemiah pursued a strategy that used a combination of organization, motivation, supervision, problem solving, and team-building skills to successfully rebuild the walls of Jerusalem in fifty-two days. His strategy is worth our study and application to our personal lives.

The successful *pray* (Nehemiah 1:4–11; 2:4, 5).

4. Two examples in the book of Nehemiah show two different styles of prayer; the first prayer was longer and intense, the other quick and to the point. What do you learn about prayer from Nehemiah's examples? _____

_____

_____

_____

The successful *obey* (Nehemiah 2:1–9).

5. Nehemiah showed submission to two authorities. Who were they and in what order did he submit? _____

_____

_____

_____

6. Nehemiah showed submission through the use of the phrase, "if it please the king" (2:5, 7). What does this attitude of submission teach you about how to submit to authority? _____

_____

_____

_____

The successful *take risks* (Nehemiah 2:10–20).

7. How large a task did Nehemiah take on? _____

_____

_____

_____

8. What did Nehemiah say to build confidence in the leaders (2:17, 18)?

_____

_____

_____

The successful *are not alone* (Nehemiah 3).

9. The phrase "next unto him," and "after him [them]" is repeated thirty times in these verses. What does this teach you about teamwork? _____

_____

_____

_____

The successful *refuse to quit* (Nehemiah 6:15–19).

Nehemiah could have quit on more than one occasion. One kind of attack came from his critics.

10. What key actions did Nehemiah take to handle this attack (4:4, 6, 9)?

_____

_____

_____

_____

11. What strategy did Nehemiah use to fight against the fear of what might happen (4:13, 14, 17, 23)? _____

_____

_____

_____

_____

12. The enemy changed its tactics (6:2, 7, 10), and Nehemiah responded (6:3, 8, 9, 11, 12). What thinking kept Nehemiah on track? _____

_____

_____

_____

13. Who did Nehemiah credit for the success of rebuilding the wall (6:16)? _____

_____

Nehemiah teaches us that God wants men to achieve the potential that He has placed within us. This potential may or may not include monetary wealth; the Bible gives examples of rich men and poor men who followed God with great success. **Real success is living a life that pleases God.** The rest of personal achievement has to do with how you faithfully manage what God has given you.

Heart Check

Do you view success from the world's view (profit, power, position) or God's view (pleasing Him)?

God-styled success is never measured by the way the culture of the world views success. God is most interested in the character of the man and that man's readiness to follow God and His purposes. God wants a man to faithfully fulfill whatever task he has before him with a heart that wants to please God.

Which of Nehemiah's strategies will help you in the challenges you are facing today? _____

_____

_____

_____

Finish the following statement for your own life: I will have succeeded when . . . _____

_____

_____

_____

Verse for Meditation

"And he shall be like a tree planted by the rivers of water, that bringeth forth his fruit in his season; his leaf also shall not wither; and whatsoever he doeth shall prosper" (Psalm 1:3).

YOUR WITNESS

Most men spend forty-plus hours a week in a place filled with people who often don't care what God thinks about work. If you work around people who are not followers of Jesus, you see every day the challenge of being a spiritual light in a dark place. Jesus taught us how important it is to be a bright light in the workplace.

"Ye are the light of the world. A city that is set on an hill cannot be hid. Neither do men light a candle, and put it under a bushel, but on a candlestick; and it giveth light unto all that are in the house. Let your light so shine before men, that they may see your good works, and glorify your Father which is in heaven" (Matthew 5:14–16).

In the Old Testament, over six hundred years before Jesus spoke about being a light in a dark place, a man named Daniel lived his life as an effective witness and worker. Early in his life he probably didn't appear to have much potential to make any kind of positive, spiritual influence on anyone. But Daniel made a remarkable transition from a "nobody slave" to a well-liked, highly respected, trusted advisor and spiritual counselor to the king.

Look at Daniel 6:20–28. What strikes you about what the Bible says about Daniel? _____

_____

_____

The next three lessons explore how Daniel, an unknown slave, became a trusted spiritual advisor to the most powerful kings on earth during that time. Every man should have these "Daniel characteristics" in order to be effective as both a worker and a witness in the workplace.

6
INTEGRITY

Integrity is an increasingly familiar word, in part because it seems to be rare in today's corporate culture. Integrity comes from the word "integer," meaning "one." Therefore, being a man of integrity means that a man is the same at work, home, and church. The opposite of a person of integrity is a hypocrite. In Greek theater a hypocrite was someone who wore a mask, pretending to be someone he was not. The challenge that a follower of Christ must accept in the workplace is to keep the same level of commitment to Christ on the job that he has at home, at church, in the community.

Few people have demonstrated integrity like Daniel. Daniel's "spiritual sameness" enabled him to be a bright witness. According to Daniel 1:1–5, Daniel's nation was conquered by Babylon when Daniel was very young. Everything was destroyed or looted. Daniel was taken into slavery and assigned to work in the king's palace. Granted, serving in the king's palace was a better assignment than the king's fields; yet it was still slavery, yielding an annual salary of zero.

An amazing series of events transpired between Daniel 1 and Daniel 6. In chapter 1 Daniel was an average slave, but by chapter 6 he was the Babylonian equivalent to the White House chief of staff. Read again Daniel 6:20–28 to see the impact of Daniel's life upon King Darius.

Daniel had an extremely visible career. He was politically connected, and he was a man of spiritual integrity. The temptation exists for each of us to think that marketplace achievement and personal integrity are mutually exclusive, but Daniel's life destroys that myth. Let's learn how Daniel developed and demonstrated his Biblical integrity.

Daniel established boundaries: integrity under temptation.

1. Read Daniel 1:1–8. What key decision did Daniel make? _____

_____

_____

_____

While Daniel excelled in his studies at the "University of Babylon," he resolved not to defile himself with the king's food and wine (v. 8). Daniel's resolution likely revolved around his commitment to Jewish dietary laws, Biblical admonitions concerning drunkenness, and the probability that the king's food and wine would have been dedicated to the idols of Babylon. Daniel had already established boundaries (what he would and would not do); so when he was tempted, he knew what to do.

2. What pressure did Daniel face to change his decision (Daniel 1:10)? _____

_____

_____

3. In what specific ways did Daniel answer the challenge (Daniel 1:11–13)? _____

_____

_____

4. How did it turn out (1:14–21)? _____

_____

_____

_____

5. Check the following challenges you have faced that required preestablished boundaries.

❏ Temptation at an office party
❏ An unethical job request from a superior
❏ Pressure to "cut corners" by fellow employees
❏ Sexually impure jokes/conversations
❏ Using company time inefficiently
❏ Other _____

6. Were you ready for the challenge? How did it turn out? _____

_____

_____

_____

Daniel embraced difficult assignments: integrity under pressure.

Daniel 2 records Nebuchadnezzar's dreams. Because of his strong desire to understand what they meant, the king went to several astrologers and insisted that they tell him what the dreams meant, "or else I'll cut you into pieces." (And you thought your boss had unrealistic expectations!) When the astrologers couldn't supply an interpretation, the king ordered all the wise men to be killed (Daniel 2:12). Daniel did not run from or complain about the unfair situation; instead he saw an opportunity to serve the Lord and Nebuchadnezzar.

7. How did Daniel respond to the king's decree (Daniel 2:14, 16)?

_____

_____

_____

_____

8. What did Daniel encourage his friends to do (2:17, 18)? _____

_____

_____

_____

Daniel developed a support structure: integrity under God and with godly men.

When Daniel was faced with the king's death sentence upon all the wise men, Daniel knew that he needed the support of other men who believed God and who would support him in prayer. Daniel asked Hananiah, Mishael, and Azariah to pray.

The Bible records other situations when one person sought the prayer support of others. On the night that Jesus was arrested, He took the disciples to Gethsemane to pray (Luke 22:39–46). When Peter was in prison, the church gathered to pray (Acts 12:5). James instructed believers to "pray one for another" (James 5:16). The discipline of depending on other Christians to pray is a vital way to maintain our spiritual integrity.

9. What happened to Daniel (Daniel 2:19–49)? _____

_____

_____

_____

Daniel revealed his spiritual commitment: integrity under the spotlight.

Daniel's commitment to God was so well-known that Daniel's co-workers plotted to outlaw prayer (Daniel 6:5–7). They were convinced that Daniel would maintain his commitment to prayer in spite of the law.

10. What did Daniel do in response to the king's "no-prayer" decree (Daniel 6:10)? _____

_____

_____

Heart Check

Take an integrity inventory and pick one area you need to develop in your life.

- What boundaries do I need to develop?
- What assignments do I need to embrace instead of complain about?
- Who is praying that I will maintain my spiritual integrity?
- In what ways can my spiritual commitment be revealed?

Daniel had a plan to meet every challenge to his integrity. He then worked his plan. Briefly outline your plan to meet challenges with integrity.

_____

_____

_____

_____

_____

Verse for Meditation

"But Daniel purposed in his heart that he would not defile himself with the portion of the king's meat, nor with the wine which he drank" (Daniel 1:8).

7
EXCELLENCE

P roverbs 6:6 and 9 speak of the "sluggard," a person who does just enough to get by, who is lazy. Today he might be called an underachiever.

Daniel was just the opposite of that description. He was marked by excellence. We can define excellence as "the commitment and determination to energetically do what is right." Our world likes to talk a lot about excellence, often using the word as a synonym for success. However, a commitment to excellence doesn't necessarily guarantee worldly success. Perhaps we can better understand excellence by seeing it at work in Daniel's life.

Daniel resisted the "good enough" attitude.

Potential is "possible productivity" that is simply wasted without action. If ever we could understand giving up, throwing in the towel, or doing just enough to get by, we see that possibility in Daniel 1. Daniel was deported as a slave. When he arrived in Babylon, he was ordered to learn the Babylonian language and all of the country's literature. What was his incentive? After all, slaves can't be demoted! Yet Daniel did his best.

1. What qualities did Daniel and his friends possess that showed

their potential (Daniel 1:4, 17)? _____

_____

_____

_____

2. What did the king think of Daniel and his friends when he reviewed their development (1:19, 20)?_____

_____

_____

_____

King Nebuchadnezzar, like many great leaders, wanted to surround himself with capable and skilled advisors. Daniel and his three friends, through their faith and obedience to God, proved themselves as superior advisors to the king. They were ready to be used to their full effectiveness by their boss. As later chapters of Daniel reveal, this pursuit of excellence on the part of Daniel and his friends made the other advisors seem rather weak; they became mad with jealousy and competition.

The purpose in pursuing excellence in our work is to bring attention and glory to God and to recognize that we are working "as to the Lord" (Colossians 3:23, 24). To pursue excellence as a means to "crush the competition" or "make it to the top" is self-centered rather than God-centered.

3. Are you pursuing excellence in your job? How would you describe your motivation to excel? _____

_____

_____

_____

4. List three past educational or training opportunities that have

helped you excel at your job. _____

_____

_____

_____

5. What training would make you more effective?

- ❏ Technical training
- ❏ Communication skills
- ❏ Organizational/time management education
- ❏ Motivational training
- ❏ Other _____

6. In what ways do the following Bible passages show commitment to pursuing excellence in work; that is, the commitment and determination to energetically do what is right?

	God's Work	Man's Work
Genesis 39:1–9	Lord was with Joseph (v. 2)	Worked hard/stayed sexually pure (vv. 8, 9)
Genesis 39:19–23		
Nehemiah 1:11		
Proverbs 22:29		
Matthew 25:14–30		
Ephesians 6:5–7		
Colossians 3:23, 24		

Daniel established balanced disciplines.

The book of Daniel provides glimpses of several disciplines in Daniel's life that supported his pursuit of excellence.

• INTELLECTUAL. Daniel was well-informed and learned a new language and the literature of a new culture (1:4).

• PHYSICAL. The Bible describes Daniel as being without physical defect. He resisted the king's food and wine, ate vegetables and drank water, and, as a result, looked healthier than all the other young men (1:4, 12, 15).

• SOCIAL. Daniel developed many positive and constructive relationships. Daniel 2:13 refers to the wise men as Daniel's friends. Daniel also had a good relationship with his boss, King Darius. King Darius anguished over sending Daniel to the lions' den and was overjoyed when he found Daniel alive the next morning (chapter 6). Daniel also developed a very supportive relationship with others who followed God; for example, his fellow captives who had been renamed Shadrach, Meshach, and Abednego (chapter 2).

• SPIRITUAL. Daniel was a model of spiritual discipline. His prayer life was so consistent that his enemies used it as a weapon against him (Daniel 6).

Achieving excellence in our work life requires a foundation of excellence in each of these areas. Jesus had this same pursuit. Luke 2:52 speaks of this balance in the growth and development of Jesus Christ, the perfect God-Man: "And Jesus increased in wisdom and stature, and in favour with God and man."

In their book *The Power of Full Engagement*, Jim Loehr and Tony Schwartz make this powerful statement about a life of balance:

"To be fully engaged, we must be physically energized, emotionally connected, mentally focused and spiritually aligned with a purpose beyond our immediate self-interest. Full engagement begins with feeling eager to get to work in the morning, equally happy to return home in the evening and capable of setting clear boundaries between the two. It means being able to immerse yourself in the mission you are on, whether that is grappling with a creative challenge at work, managing a group of people on a project, spending time with loved ones or simply having fun" *(The Power of Full Engagement* [New York: Simon and Schuster, 2002], 5, 6).

When you consider all the people your life touches at work, at home, in your neighborhood, in your community, in your church, each detail should draw attention to the Author of the light within you, Jesus Christ.

7. According to Matthew 5:14–16, what will make people see the light? _____

_____

Heart Check

What *action* do you need to take this week to pursue godly excellence?

_____

_____

_____

Verse for Meditation

"And Jesus increased in wisdom and stature, and in favour with God and man" (Luke 2:52).

8
COURAGE

Courage is not being fearless; rather, it is knowing the risk (and even feeling the fear) but going ahead anyway because it's the right thing to do. Daniel wasn't larger than life or fearless; but he was courageous. Let's notice two characteristics of courage from his life.

Daniel maintained unpopular convictions.

We learned in Lesson 6 that when Daniel was served the king's food and wine, he faced a tough choice. He knew that eating the king's food was wrong, but how would he handle the situation? Should he conclude that since he was in Babylon, he should do as the Babylonians did?

More than a few Christians use difficulty and marketplace obligations as an excuse for disobedience. Have you ever dropped your napkin in order to camouflage a prayer at a business lunch?

Daniel did not loudly quote the dietary laws of the Pentateuch or criticize the Babylonians for eating such things. That would have been offensive, not courageous.

Instead, Daniel asked permission to not eat the king's food. He handled his Biblical convictions politely and respectfully.

Note the difference between courage and stubbornness. Courage stands up for what is Biblically right; stubbornness stands up for personal preferences.

1. How does Daniel 2:1–30 indicate Daniel's courage?_____

_____

_____

_____

2. What was the result of that courageous encounter (2:46–49)?

_____

_____

_____

Daniel withstood painful consequences.

For the courageous person, doing the right thing is more powerful than the risk involved. Daniel knew about the legal ban on prayer, and he knew the penalty (Daniel 6:1–10).

3. Everything worked out positively when Daniel refused to eat from the king's table. What happened to Daniel this time (Daniel 6:11–17)? _____

_____

_____

_____

4. Has your employer asked you to do something that is outside Biblical boundaries? How did you handle the situation?_____

_____

_____

Oftentimes what opens the ears of those whom God wants us to influence is the demonstration of Biblical courage.

Courage on display #1

5. Consider what happened to Daniel's friends when they showed courage through their active faith. What did Nebuchadnezzar want them to do (Daniel 3:8–15, 19–23)? _____

_____

_____

_____

_____

_____

6. How did they respond (3:16–18)? _____

_____

_____

_____

7. What was the result according to Daniel 3:24–30? _____

_____

_____

_____

Courage on display #2

Bill was a salesman for a large food-service corporation. When he took the multistate sales region, he was told that he would be expected to "wine and dine" the clients in this region if he wanted to meet the expected sales figures. Respectfully and wisely, Bill talked with his superior, explaining his Christian convictions. Bill presented a plan for achieving the desired sales figures without the "wine and dine" expectation. As Bill prayed and pursued with excellence his sales region, God brought about success so that his sales figures were greater than anyone else on the sales force and far exceeded the company's expectations. Bill's courage made the difference.

Courage on display #3

Scott worked as an insurance salesman. His manager used the lure of all-expenses-paid family trips and prizes to motivate his sales force toward higher sales for the company. Scott was already leading his sales region in policies sold and was convinced in his own heart that the "trips-and-prizes" motivation caused his own focus to turn toward a what's-in-this-for-me attitude. Scott presented a plan to his manager that would meet his manager's expectations of phone calls and contacts but would excuse Scott from participation in the "drive-for-the-trip" program. His boss accepted his plan, and Scott exceeded the manager's sales goals. He would have qualified to win the trip, but he did not go.

Heart Check

Do you have a story of courage on display? What is it?_____

_____

_____

_____

How many people where you work know about your commitment to God?

_____ no one _____ a few _____ everyone who knows me

Identify how you reveal your commitment to Christ when you are at work.

- ❏ Place tracts and information about Christ in various locations
- ❏ Be quiet about my faith and hope someone notices a different attitude
- ❏ Invite people to church or "Christian" events
- ❏ Show true concern for people's lives
- ❏ Find ways to serve my fellow workers
- ❏ Pray before I eat meals
- ❏ Make sure my speech patterns are godly and consistent
- ❏ Do right—respectfully but firmly—when confronted with a compromising decision

Verses for Meditation

"Ye are the salt of the earth. . . . Ye are the light of the world. . . . Let your light so shine before men, that they may see your good works, and glorify your Father which is in heaven" (Matthew 5:13, 14, 16).

WRAP-UP

God is a vital part of your job. The goal of this study has been to discover the importance of your job in God's plan for your life. Too many men try to divide their lives into secular and sacred slices, with work being part of the secular. These lessons have helped you learn that work is a sacred calling from God.

The principles in this study are meant to be a guide and resource for the rest of your life. As you encounter challenges at work, a hard-to-get-along-with boss, a difficult coworker, or the need to transition to a new role, go back and review the principles and Bible passages in this study.

From this day forward, refuse to merely endure the time *at* work; rather, embrace God's plan *for* your work.

RESOURCES FOR FURTHER STUDY

Hendricks, William, and Doug Sherman. *How to Balance Competing Time Demands.* Colorado Springs: NavPress, 1989.

Hendricks, William, and Doug Sherman. *Your Work Matters to God.* Colorado Springs: NavPress, 1987.

Hughes, R. Kent. *Disciplines of a Godly Man.* Wheaton, Ill.: Crossway Books, 1991.

Swenson, Richard. *Margin: Restoring Emotional, Physical, Financial, and Time Reserves to Overloaded Lives.* Colorado Springs: NavPress, 1992.